August
AN AFTERNOON IN THE COUNTRY

August

AN AFTERNOON IN THE COUNTRY

By Jean Marc Dalpé

Translated by Maureen Labonté

Playwrights Canada Press
Toronto • Canada

Août, Un repas à la campagne © Copyright 2006 Jean Marc Dalpé
August, An Afternoon in the Country (translation) ©
Copyright 2007 Maureen Labonté
The moral rights of the authors are asserted.
French text copyright © 2006 by Éditions Prise de parole, Ottawa. All rights reserved.
First published in French as *Août: Un repas à la campagne* by Éditions Prise de parole, Ottawa.

Playwrights Canada Press
The Canadian Drama Publisher
215 Spadina Avenue, Suite 230, Toronto, Ontario CANADA M5T 2C7
416-703-0013 fax 416-408-3402
orders@playwrightscanada.com • www.playwrightscanada.com

CAUTION: This play is fully protected under the copyright laws of Canada and all other countries of the Copyright Union, and is subject to royalty. Changes to the script are expressly forbidden without the prior written permission of the author. Rights to produce, film, or record, in whole or in part, in any medium or any language, by any group, amateur or professional, are retained by the author, who has the right to grant or refuse permission at the time of the request. For professional or amateur production rights, please contact: Catherine Mensour, The Mensour Agency, 41 Springfield Road, Ottawa, Ontario, K1M 1C8, 613-241-1677, kate@mensour.ca.

No part of this book, covered by the copyright hereon, may be reproduced or used in any form or by any means—graphic, electronic or mechanical—without the prior written permission of the publisher except for excerpts in a review. Any request for photocopying, recording, taping or information storage and retrieval systems of any part of this book shall be directed in writing to Access Copyright, 1 Yonge Street, Suite 800, Toronto, Ontario CANADA M5E 1E5 416-868-1620.

This book would be twice its cover price were it not for the support of Canadian taxpayers through the Government of Canada Book Publishing Industry Development Programme, the Canada Council for the Arts, the Ontario Arts Council, and the Ontario Media Development Corporation.

 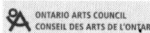

Front cover painting "L'essouflement" by Marie-Doris Valois www.mariedorisvalois.com
Production Editor/Cover Design: JLArt

Library and Archives Canada Cataloguing in Publication

Dalpé, Jean-Marc, 1957-
[Août. English]
    August : an afternoon in the country / by Jean Marc Dalpé ; translated by Maureen Labonté.

A play.
Translation of: Août : un repas à la campagne.
ISBN 978-0-88754-506-1

    I. Labonté, Maureen, 1949- II. Titre. III. Titre: Août. English.

PS8557.A458A8813 2007   C842'.54   C2007-906248-2

First edition: November 2007.
Printed and bound by AGMV Marquis at Quebec, Canada.

For
Robert Dickson
(1944 - 2007)

And addiction stays on tight like a glove.[1]

Daniel Lanois

---

[1] From the song "Where Will I Be," sung by Emmylou Harris on her CD, *Wrecking Ball*.

Acknowledgements

I would like to thank Bob White, Artistic Director of Alberta Theatre Projects for his love of this play and support of the English translation. Thanks also to ATP's Dianne Goodman and Vicki Stroich and to everyone who worked on the workshop and reading of *August* at ATP in March of 2007 – Vanessa Porteous, Amy-Lynn Strilchuk, Brian Dooley, Nancy Beattie, Irene Poole, Valerie Planche, John Kirkpatrick, Grant Linneberg, Elinor Holt and Gemma James-Smith.

My heartfelt thanks also go to Colleen Murphy and Linda Gaboriau for their friendship and support.

And finally, love and very special thanks to my daughter, Marielle. This one's for you!

—M.L.

Setting

A large, run-down farmhouse.

The front veranda is listing slightly forward. On it, there's an old dog house, a pair of rubber boots, two old metal garden chairs, a low table and a two-seater swing.

Everything is a bit rusty.

The front entrance leads to the main part of the house. There are in fact two doors – a screen door which opens out and a solid, massive, wooden inner door which will remain open for most of the play.

The window by the swing is the living-room window.

To the side of the house, stage right, there's an old apple tree which we don't see but which provides shade. There are a few rotten apples on the ground.

In front, there's a small stretch of lawn which gives onto a dirt driveway where the cars are parked. This means that the characters make entrances and exits through the audience.

A path on the stage-left side of the house leads to the barn, the garage and the other farm outbuildings.

Time

Late on a Saturday afternoon. Around 4:30p.m.

Mid-August.

The third day of a heat wave.

The Prologue takes place the evening before.

Notes on the Text

A " / " in a line of dialogue indicates when the next character should start speaking. The two lines overlap.

Lines in parenthesis are meant to be more introspective, as if the characters were speaking to themselves but out loud.

The playwright uses "…" (the ellipsis) in two different ways. Firstly, to indicate a line or word that trails off or an incomplete sentence. Secondly, and this is a little more unusual, at the end of a line *and* the beginning of the same character's next line to signal that the sentence keeps rolling without a pause while other dialogue fits under or over.

Note to Producers

As this text went to press before the premiere production of the English translation, please consult with the playwright and translator, their agent (whose contact information may be found on the copyright page), or the publisher for the most recent version of the script.

Août, Un repas à la campagne, produced by the Théâtre de La Manufacture, premiered on April 11, 2006, at the Théâtre de la Licorne in Montreal with the following company:

Louise	Annick Bergeron
Gabriel	Henri Chassé
Simon	Pierre Curzi
Josée	Catherine de Léan
Jeanne	Louise Laprade
André Mathieu	Jacques L'Heureux
Paulette	Janine Sutto
Monique	Marie Tifo

Directed by Fernand Rainville
Assistant to the Director: Allain Roy
Set design by Patricia Ruel
Costume design by Mirielle Vachon
Lighting design by André Rioux
Sound design by Larsen Lupin
Props by Marie-Ève Lemieux
Makeup by Suzanne Trépanier
Wigs by Cybèles Perruques

— • —

August, An Afternoon in the Country was commissioned by Alberta Theatre Projects. The translation was workshopped and read as a Platform Reading during ATP's annual Enbridge playRites Festival in February, 2007. Vanessa Porteous directed the reading which featured Nancy Beattie (Jeanne), Brian Dooley (Simon), Elinor Holt (Monique), Gemma James-Smith (Josée), John Kirkpatrick (André Mathieu), Grant Linneberg (Gaby), Valerie Planche (Paulette) and Irene Poole (Louise).

Characters

LOUISE   "Lou-Lou." The wife. 38 years old. Summer dress. Blue streaks in her hair.

GABRIEL   "Gab" or "Gaby." The husband. 42 years old. Jeans. A white t-shirt. Work boots. Baseball cap.

JOSÉE   Their daughter. 19 years old. Sporty mid-calf designer pants. A camisole. A baseball cap. Her navel is pierced.

SIMON   Louise's father. 57 years old. Still suffering from the after-effects of a major stroke he had three years earlier, as well as from recent radiation treatments for throat cancer. He drinks constantly from a water bottle.

JEANNE   Louise's mother. 60 years old. At the beginning of the play, she wears an apron over her "Sunday dress." Her hair is dyed; the roots are grey.

PAULETTE   Jeanne's mother. 86 years old. Men's glasses. A hearing aid. She walks slowly. Uses a cane she doesn't really need.

MONIQUE   Simon's sister. 58 years old. Some men would say she's "well-preserved," most women that she "works hard at it." A little too much make-up. A little too much jewellery.

ANDRÉ MATHIEU   Her fiancé. 57 years old. Hair dyed black. The golfer-look. Short-sleeved Lacoste shirt, well-pressed trousers, comfortable leather shoes.

August
An Afternoon in the Country

PRE-SHOW

While the audience enters and gets settled, we hear a selection of songs by Willie Nelson ("Teatro," "Love Songs"), Merle Haggard ("If I Could Only Fly"), and Emmylou Harris ("Wrecking Ball," "Red Dirt Girl")…

Love songs. Songs about love going bad. Hurtin' songs.

GABRIEL is working. He's repairing one of the steps leading up to the veranda. He rips off the rotten wood, takes measurements and then, with an electric round saw, cuts pieces of treated wood, fits them and nails them into place.

Once the job is done, he tidies up. He gathers the wood he didn't use and puts it and his tools away as the music fades and the lights slowly go to black.

PROLOGUE

We hear a few short, sharp toots of a car horn in the distance. From a car passing by along the concession road in front of the house. The car approaches and then drives off.

The rhythm of the horn toots is a rather happy one, as if the driver wanted to be recognized and assumed that he would be.

But GABRIEL doesn't seem to recognize the car.

Once the car has driven off, GABRIEL is about to exit toward the barn when LOUISE, in a skirt and blouse, enters from inside the house carrying a small document case and a pair of high-heeled shoes which she will put on during the scene.

As she sits down on the steps GABRIEL has just repaired:

LOUISE
I'm taking the truck. Do you have the keys?
(GABRIEL seems to hesitate. LOUISE holds up the document case.)
That young couple who saw the Lapierre's house at the beginning of the week want to make an offer, but they'd like to have another look at it first. The young couple from Nova Scotia…? From Halifax…? The wife's pregnant…? *(GABRIEL nods.)* They want to ask me a few questions, talk to me. Want to be reassured. The guy mostly. She seems to have made up her mind, but the guy…?

GABRIEL
Maybe after…? Would you like to go for a swim at the quarry? We haven't been yet this year? *(He moves over to her.)* Just you and me? *(He reaches out to touch her arm.)* You, me, and the moon?

LOUISE steps back before he can touch her.

LOUISE
It'll be too late.

She's finished putting on her shoes and stands up.

GABRIEL
I'm trying to…

LOUISE *(interrupting him, very brusque)*
I know. I got that.
(then, trying to make amends)
Sorry.

GABRIEL *(as he gives her the keys to the truck)*
Even if you get back late, we could still head over?

LOUISE *(without looking him in the eyes)*
You're trying to go too fast. Gotta give it time. It's not something you can just switch off.

She heads off quickly in the direction of the driveway and the parked cars. A moment later, JEANNE arrives at the screen door. She stands there and talks to GABRIEL from inside.

JEANNE
She going out?

> *During the next few lines we hear the sounds of the truck starting up and driving off.*

GABRIEL
Your daughter's maybe gonna sell a house tonight.

JEANNE
Which one?

GABRIEL
The Lapierre's.

JEANNE
That was sold two days ago. I talked to Hélène this morning. Their house was sold two days ago. Sold. Signed.

> *The truck is gone.*

GABRIEL
I musta gotten it wrong.

JEANNE
I can call Hélène, if you want.
Gaby?
I'll go call Hélène.

> *JEANNE moves away from the door and heads inside.*
> *GABRIEL doesn't move.*
> *Like a man who knows he should do something but who doesn't know how.*
> *Not yet.*
> *Then, the lights suddenly snap to black.*

AUGUST

MONIQUE is sitting on the swing fanning herself with a travel brochure.

Behind her, in the living room, we can barely see PAULETTE who's sitting listening to gospel music ("Will the Circle Be Unbroken," the original version from the 30s sung by The Carter Family). We hear the music playing softly in the background because the window is slightly open. An electric fan has been placed close to the window and it's turning. Not making too much noise.

MONIQUE *(talking in the direction of the house)*
I think Louise's blue streaks look really good on her. Whoa… blue!!

A short pause. Same routine.

"Not her age," that's nonsense. (Utter nonsense.[2]) And, coming from someone like Fabienne! The nerve of her to say that to you – okay, it's not all that surprising now that she is who she is and all – but coming from her…
(She laughs. Then, with a sigh:)
I'd like to remind her of one or two little "incidents" in her life… ay, Jeanne?… ay?… when the opinions… when the judgement/ [3] of other women…

JOSÉE *(from inside the house)*
It's not there.

JEANNE *(from inside)*
You didn't find it?

JOSÉE *(from inside)*
No.

MONIQUE *(same as before)*
What's important is that she likes it. What someone like Fabienne thinks whether she's the wife / of an MP or not, I…

JEANNE *(inside)*
Go without the bill, he'll find your uniform for you.

---

[2] Lines or parts of lines in parenthesis indicate a change of tone, often more introspective.
[3] A " / " indicates an overlap, where the next line begins.

JOSÉE enters from the house holding her wallet in her hand.

JOSÉE *(to MONIQUE)*
I don't have it.

MONIQUE
Oh.

JOSÉE
It's weird.

JEANNE *(inside)*
Tell him who you are.

JOSÉE *(to JEANNE inside)*
He'd do it for you, Gran, 'cause he knows you. But he doesn't know me.
(to MONIQUE)
He doesn't know me. The man at the dry cleaners doesn't know me.
(to JEANNE, inside)
I know you're right. And if I don't have a choice, but y'know… shit.
(Shit.)

MONIQUE
Go without it. Happens all the time.

JOSÉE
It's because… there's a phone number… I wrote a phone number on the back. My producer's number. (Well… the producer who could become my producer.)
(MONIQUE seems not to understand.)
The one from the contest…? My screenplay…?
(MONIQUE still doesn't seem to get what she's talking about.)
My mother didn't tell you?
(MONIQUE shakes her head.)
(Christ.)

MONIQUE
You won a contest?

JOSÉE
I'm a finalist. There are twenty finalists and they choose five. The five short films they pick get made. And they're deciding this weekend. Like now. Like right now. My mother didn't tell you?

(MONIQUE shakes her head.)
It's just like, you know, maybe the most important thing that could happen to me in my entire life!

JEANNE *(from inside)*
Josée? You still there?

JOSÉE *(to JEANNE)*
Yes!

JEANNE *(from inside)*
Don't forget the money for the raspberries.

JOSÉE *(to JEANNE)*
I've got it.

JEANNE *(from inside)*
You have enough?

JOSÉE *(like a threat)*
I'm not going to the Rioux's.

JEANNE *(from inside)*
The ones from the store will do fine.

JOSÉE
They'll have to 'cause I'm not going to the Rioux's.

JEANNE *(from inside)*
But don't pay more than three dollars a basket! That's already highway robbery.

JOSÉE *(to MONIQUE)*
I can see myself putting it on my desk. Clear as day.

MONIQUE
It's so annoying when that happens.

JOSÉE
(Clear.)

MONIQUE
You can't stop thinking about it.

JOSÉE
(I don't understand.)

MONIQUE
You start to get upset! Well, I do. Really upset. (Makes me crazy.) And you start looking everywhere…

JOSÉE
I did. I looked everywhere. / I looked…

MONIQUE
You look and look…

JOSÉE
Everywhere. Even in places it couldn't be. Even though I knew I wouldn't find it, that it made no sense.

MONIQUE
And you don't look just once. Oh no…! You look everywhere. You stop. And then you start all over again. It's the third time you've gone through the same drawer or looked behind the couch / but…

JOSÉE
Hm…

MONIQUE
…until you find it… ay?

> *A short pause. Then, JOSÉE starts going through her wallet again. MONIQUE turns back toward the house.*

Jeanne?

JOSÉE *(about her search)*
I don't know why I'm doing this.

MONIQUE *(to the inside of the house)*
Jeanne?

JEANNE
Yes?

MONIQUE *(to JEANNE inside)*
I'm not going to ask again. Do you need help?

JEANNE *(from inside)*
No, thanks.

MONIQUE *(to JEANNE)*
I won't ask again.

> *JOSÉE has finished looking through her wallet. Then, with a small cry of frustration, she throws the wallet onto the low table.*

JOSÉE
I see it. In my hand.

MONIQUE
Okay.

JOSÉE
I've just written down the number.

MONIQUE
Yeah…

JOSÉE
I'm in my room and I say to myself…

MONIQUE
I know…

JOSÉE
As I put it down on the desk… I see myself. I see myself doing it. It's so clear! (Fuck!)… and I say to myself / …(I don't understand, I just don't understand.)

MONIQUE
As you put it down on the desk, you said to yourself, "This way I won't forget it."

JOSÉE
This way, I won't lose it.

MONIQUE
"When the time comes and I need it…"

JOSÉE
(Like now, Christ! Like now.)

MONIQUE
…but when you reach for what you know should be right there…. Gone!

JOSÉE
It's in my hand. I put it down on the desk.

MONIQUE
"What's going on? What happened?"

JOSÉE
I don't know.

MONIQUE
"But... I'm sure I..."

JOSÉE
Absolutely sure. Because it's my place! It's the place where I always put like, like things like that, like.... Right beside the phone with my to-do list. It's my place for, for all the...

MONIQUE
For the things you want to be able to find...

JOSÉE
...'cause you know you're going to need them the next day. It's my special place! So why didn't I do it? I knew I'd need it today. If I don't have my uniform, I don't work. Why wouldn't I have put it there?!

MONIQUE
Because something distracted you...?

JOSÉE
I'd remember.

MONIQUE
A phone call...?

JOSÉE
I'd remember.

MONIQUE
You were about to put it down and...

JOSÉE
No. No, I'd remember. I mean, it's possible. It is possible, but... I guess it has to be that, 'cause otherwise the bill would be there. And, since it's not... I moved it later.

MONIQUE
Ah.

JOSÉE
I put it somewhere else?

MONIQUE
You or someone else...

JOSÉE
I thought of that, but no one goes into my room. No one.

MONIQUE
Things don't just disappear. Poof! There's always an explanation.

JOSÉE
I clean my own room. (My room is my room.)

MONIQUE
Okay, you clean it. But if / you...

JOSÉE
Except...

MONIQUE
Ah.

JOSÉE
I'm going to go ask my mother. She uses my computer sometimes. To go on the net.

MONIQUE
Ah!

JOSÉE exits quickly in the direction of the barn.

JOSÉE
But like... why would she take it? A bill...?

MONIQUE
There's always an explanation.

JOSÉE is gone, but MONIQUE keeps talking to her.

A mystery is a mystery until it's not a mystery anymore. And then...! I love that feeling. It's so great!

MONIQUE laughs to herself. Then, like the night before, we hear a series of toots from a car as it drives by on the concession road. MONIQUE looks off into the distance, waves, but clearly has no idea who it is.

Jeanne?

>   *Short pause. Then she glances through the window to the living room and, raising her voice, calls inside.*

Jeanne?

JEANNE *(from inside)*
Yes?

MONIQUE
Um... is Paulette...?

JEANNE *(from inside)*
Yes?

MONIQUE
Is she coming?

JEANNE *(from inside)*
She invited?

MONIQUE
Course she is.

JEANNE *(from inside)*
Ask her.

>   *As she turns her head toward the window, MONIQUE sniffs because she notices (or thinks she notices) that she smells of sweat. Without missing a beat in the following dialogue, she takes a bottle of cologne out of her purse and sprays herself. After she puts it back in her purse, she realizes that her hands are damp and sticky. She takes out a case with wet-towels and uses one to wipe her hands.*

MONIQUE *(to JEANNE)*
You know about the room at the hotel after the reception...?

JEANNE *(from inside)*
We've already settled that, Monique.

MONIQUE
You told us. I know. But it's not just a room anymore, it's a suite.

JEANNE *(from inside)*
Doesn't change a thing.

MONIQUE
It's a suite. André saw it.

JEANNE
Doesn't change a thing.

MONIQUE
It's just that... we said to ourselves, if your mother comes to the wedding... is she coming?

JEANNE *(from inside)*
Ask her. Isn't she with you?

MONIQUE
She's in the living room.

JEANNE *(from inside)*
What's she doing in the living room?

MONIQUE
She's listening to her music.

JEANNE *(from inside)*
She's crazy. It must be a hundred in there.
She's crazy.
It's the worst room in the house when it's hot like this.

MONIQUE
You never had air conditioning put in, eh?

JEANNE *(from inside)*
What?

MONIQUE
Air conditioning.

JEANNE *(from inside)*
We wouldn't use it.

MONIQUE
You would today.
Jeanne?

JEANNE *(from inside)*
Yes?

MONIQUE
I said, you'd use it on a day like today.
At my place – a day like today? – without it... (oh Jesus). It's hot here but in the city... (Downtown, it must be...)

At André's it's part of the heating system. You know… what are they called those systems? You never open a window, summer or winter.

JEANNE *(inside)*
That at André's?

MONIQUE
Oh, what's it called?

JEANNE *(inside the house)*
It'll be your house soon.
Funny. You never had a good thing to say about the suburbs.

MONIQUE
It's a package deal, Jeanne. Can't have one without the other.

JEANNE *(from inside)*
Weren't you supposed to talk him into living downtown?

MONIQUE
I tried.

JEANNE *(from inside)*
Is he stubborn?

MONIQUE
You could say that. He's a man of his generation.

> *She knocks on the living room window. Then she signals to PAULETTE.*

JEANNE *(from inside)*
You two are going to swelter tomorrow!

MONIQUE
What? What did you say?

JEANNE *(from inside)*
You're going to swelter tomorrow.

MONIQUE
On the golf course?

JEANNE *(from inside)*
You're going to swelter.

MONIQUE
Tell me about it.
(to PAULETTE)

Come join us. Outside. Come outside.
(She leans down in order to speak through the opening.)
You're covered in perspiration. Come get some air.

PAULETTE turns off the fan.

PAULETTE
What?

MONIQUE
The living room is like an oven. Come sit out here.

PAULETTE turns the music down.

PAULETTE
What?

MONIQUE
Aren't you hot?

PAULETTE
I've got my fan.

MONIQUE
It's cooler out here.

Short pause.

PAULETTE
Okay.

MONIQUE
You're coming out?

PAULETTE
I'll finish listening to this song.

MONIQUE
I want to invite you to my wedding.

Short pause.

PAULETTE
Okay.

PAULETTE turns up the volume of her music. JEANNE arrives from the house with a pitcher of lemonade and two glasses on a tray.

JEANNE
How d'you find the little one?

MONIQUE
Louise?

JEANNE
Josée.

> *As she puts the tray down on the table, JEANNE notices JOSÉE's wallet and thinking JOSÉE has left without it, she slips it into the pocket of her apron.*

MONIQUE
She's pretty as a picture. Were we ever pretty like that, Jeanne? Young, pretty, thin….

JEANNE
"Thin"? Don't talk about "thin," Monique.
(MONIQUE looks baffled.)
Monique! "Thin"?! She had us real worried with all that business.

MONIQUE
Oh my, that's true.

JEANNE
We were very, very worried.

> *JEANNE pours lemonade into the two glasses.*

MONIQUE
Oh my dear, it's an epidemic. There was an article about it in *Chatelaine*. A few years back. *Chatelaine* or that French magazine there…?

JEANNE
Elle?

MONIQUE
Or both? Mighta been both.
(JEANNE goes back into the house. MONIQUE continues, louder.)
They're not talking about it as much anymore. Those sicknesses go in and out of fashion. Everybody's talking about them and then, no one is. In and out of fashion.
(Except for cancer. That's always in fashion.)

> *JEANNE comes back out with ice which she adds to their two glasses. As she hands one of the glasses to MONIQUE:*

JEANNE
At any rate, she's stopped making herself vomit.

MONIQUE
Good. That's encouraging.

JEANNE
Except they warned us it could start again. That's why we didn't want her to go to college in town this year. But she's nineteen, she thinks she knows everything, the schools out here aren't good enough, they don't have the film courses she wants to take. And, expensive! Her father wanted to keep her here, but Louise said… "No. No, we'll manage."

> *They drink. As soon as she tastes it…*

It's sour.

MONIQUE
It's not.

JEANNE
It's sour.

> *JEANNE starts to get up to go back into the house.*

MONIQUE
You're doing too much.

JEANNE *(as she enters the house)*
Don't drink it. Wait.

MONIQUE *(to JEANNE in the house)*
Jeanne…
(Oh, Jeanne…)
You're the one I'm worried about right now. You're doing too much. I'm not talking about the lemonade, I'm talking about all the rest: your mother, my brother…
Did you hear back about your blood pressure?

> *JEANNE comes back out with the sugar bowl.*

JEANNE
My pressure's been good ever since the doctor changed my pills.

> JEANNE picks up MONIQUE's glass. During the exchange that follows, she will add sugar to both glasses and taste the lemonade a number of times until she's completely satisfied with the results.

MONIQUE
You're thinner.
That's not a good sign. At our age, losing weight can mean a lot of things.

JEANNE
That's not it.

MONIQUE
You've got to realize that you're carrying a lot on those shoulders of yours: your mother who's... what? Eighty?

JEANNE
Eighty-six.

MONIQUE
Your husband who / can't do what he—

JEANNE
That's not it. And, believe me, if I'm saying that's not it, it's because / I know that...

MONIQUE
You need a break.

JEANNE
Hah! There's no rest for the wicked.

MONIQUE *(She laughs.)*
Oh Jeanne. I haven't heard that in ages.

> JEANNE pours them some more lemonade.

JEANNE
No rest for the wicked. *(She smiles.)* My grandmother used to say that.

> They drink.

MONIQUE
Take two, three days next week and come spend them with me in town.

(All through this speech, JEANNE keeps refusing, shaking her head and her hands...)
Jeanne. André's going to California to see his grandchildren. And I'm going to be all alone. He's there for at least ten days to help his son with the new baby. Do it for me.

JEANNE
Thank you, but...

MONIQUE
You want to. I know you want to. And I also know / that you...

JEANNE
I really can't. Not right now.

MONIQUE
Louise can look after whatever needs looking after. Josée can help.

JEANNE
Josée's useless. All she does is read all day or watch movies. And Louise...

MONIQUE
Louise is more than capable of covering for you. Two or three days, Jeanne.

JEANNE
Thank you for the invitation, but not right now... / Really...

MONIQUE
"Not right now"...!

JEANNE
Really, I can't / take the—

MONIQUE
"Not right now." That, dear, is classic. Classic *burn-out!* It's what every woman says...

JEANNE
(Oh Monique...)

MONIQUE
...says when she refuses to recognize...

JEANNE
(Just because you...)

MONIQUE
...the signs. I can't tell you how many times I've seen it in the department.

JEANNE
You don't know. You don't know what you're talking about. You don't.

MONIQUE
Say "yes."

JEANNE
I've read the articles too. We do get magazines out here, you know.

MONIQUE
Say "yes," say "yes," say "yes"...

JEANNE
I can't see myself, / no...

MONIQUE
Say "yes," I'll come get you and drive you back. You won't have to do a thing. I'll take care of everything. Absolutely everything. We'll go out. We won't cook for the entire two days. We won't touch a dish, a dustcloth, a broom. We're steppin' out, girl!

JEANNE
I can't accept.

MONIQUE
Not a word about money.

JEANNE
I don't have the kind of money / you have. I never have had...

MONIQUE
Hush. Not a word. Do it for me. Please. Make me happy, Jeanne. Let me spoil you. Let your sister-in-law / really spoil you...

JEANNE
Spoil me...!

MONIQUE
...for two whole days. It'll make me so happy.

JEANNE
I couldn't. I'd / feel as though...

MONIQUE
Nonsense. That's ridiculous. If someone offers you a gift...

JEANNE
I know, I know.

MONIQUE
...a gift, no strings attached...

JEANNE
It's just that we've had to be so careful / the last few years...

MONIQUE
But what I'm saying to you... listen to me, Jeanne...

JEANNE
Things are better, now.

MONIQUE
I know. With Louise selling houses. I know.

JEANNE
A lot better.

MONIQUE
All I'm saying is, put yourself first. That's not a sin anymore and, and... oh, take a friggin' break why don't you!
(A short pause.)
You're allowed!

JEANNE pours herself another glass of lemonade.

JEANNE
If we do it in two weeks, that'll be right before the little one starts college, I could go up to town with her and help her move / into her new apartment and then...

MONIQUE
No, no, no. (Damn it!) Jeanne.... Time for you...

JEANNE
Okay.

MONIQUE
For... / you...

JEANNE
Yes. Okay.

> *(She spills her lemonade all over herself.)*

Okay! Oh!
(JEANNE bursts into tears but, just as quickly, gets herself under control again.)
You see how tired I am.

> Pause.

MONIQUE
That's what I've been saying.

> *JEANNE gets up and goes back into the house.*
> Pause.

(toward the house)
Don't forget, you'll be making me happy too.

> *JOSÉE enters quickly from the direction of the barn. She's carrying a sawhorse, one of two that will be used to make the table for dinner.*

So?

JOSÉE
It was her. It's in her purse / by the door.

MONIQUE
There you go.

JOSÉE
She took it yesterday because she was going into the village, and… duh! She forgot about it!

> *She looks around trying to find where to put the sawhorse.*
> *JEANNE enters with a cloth.*

JEANNE
How come you're still here? D'you know what time it is?

JOSÉE
What? I've / got lotsa time to…

JEANNE
It's Saturday. Saturday.

JOSÉE
Shit.

JEANNE
The cleaner closes at / five o'clock.

JOSÉE
At five! I forgot! Oh! The keys! Where're the keys! The keys!...

> *JOSÉE drops the sawhorse and rushes into the house repeating "the keys"... while JEANNE lifts her apron to show MONIQUE the stain on her dress.*

JEANNE
I'll have to change.

> *Then, she starts to clean up the mess she made around the chair and the table.*

MONIQUE *(without moving)*
Gimme. I'll / do that.

JEANNE
I don't know what I'll wear. No matter how many loads of washing you do, there never seems to be an end to it especially in weather like this.

JOSÉE *(from inside)*
My money! Where's my money! / My money!...

JEANNE *(toward the house)*
Here. Your money's here!

> *JEANNE has finished wiping up and turns to go back into the house as JOSÉE comes out with her mother's purse in her hand.*

JOSÉE
I'll be okay, they never really close before... hey! Where's my money!? Come on, this isn't funny!

> *JEANNE comes back outside without the cloth and takes the wallet out of her apron pocket.*

JEANNE
Take it! Here! It was me. I've got it.

JOSÉE
Fuck, Gran!

JEANNE
Your language, young lady.

> *JOSÉE rushes out toward the driveway and the cars, but stops suddenly.*

JOSÉE
Shit. The car. (What else is new? The car…)

> *JOSÉE changes direction and heads toward the barn.*

The car. (Fuck!) Fuck! It's always the same around here! Mister…? Mister what's-his-name! His car's blocking the way out!!…

MONIQUE
Josée, come back here! Come back! I've got a key.

> *JOSÉE crosses to MONIQUE who's going through her purse looking for the key.*

JEANNE
If you're late, it'll / be your own fault not anyone else's.

JOSÉE
I know, I know.

JEANNE
Don't blame other people because you…

MONIQUE *(to JOSÉE)*
It's here somewhere, it's right here…

JOSÉE
Grandma, how long've we been talking about widening the driveway? It's always the same "Move the car, I've got to get out! Move the pick-up! Move the car!" I thought it was funny when I was little, before I got my license, but now / it's a…

JEANNE
Shshsh.

JOSÉE
It's a pain in the ass…

JEANNE
Shshshsh.

JOSÉE
Must be… what?… six, seven years at least and still nothing's been

done. *(to MONIQUE)* Look at this place! It's a total mess! Nothing works, everything's falling apart! It's crazy...
(as she takes the key that MONIQUE is holding out to her:)
Thanks.
(as she heads off in the direction of the cars:)
Like... everyone around here... like, like it doesn't bother them to live like this! Makes no sense! Why not just do what needs to be done!
(She turns to JEANNE and MONIQUE before leaving.)
A decent place to park! Enough room for... we have two vehicles, how complicated is that?!
(as she's exiting:)
(Goddam place... drives me crazy...)

>*The two women laugh. Then JEANNE goes back into the house and MONIQUE finishes her glass of lemonade. PAULETTE enters from the living room but stays inside the screen door. As she goes to pour herself another glass of lemonade, MONIQUE notices her.*

MONIQUE
Ah, good.

>*PAULETTE opens the door, moves slightly forward but still doesn't come outside. MONIQUE pours the lemonade.*

PAULETTE
My chair's not out there.

MONIQUE
There are two here.

PAULETTE
I don't like those chairs. I prefer mine.

MONIQUE
You have a special chair?

>*PAULETTE looks at something (her folding lawn chair) that's just inside the door.*

PAULETTE
Not special. Just a chair.

MONIQUE
You don't like the swing?

> *PAULETTE points to her chair.*

PAULETTE
It's this one here. They bring it in at night. (I don't know why.)

MONIQUE
D'you want me to bring it out for you?

> *PAULETTE comes out onto the veranda.*

PAULETTE
Yes. It pinched me real good once.
(*MONIQUE goes and gets the chair.*)
Made me bleed. (But I still like it.)

MONIQUE
I'll just move one of these over here like / this, you'll be able to…

PAULETTE
No, no. In the shade.

> *PAULETTE points to the apple tree, stage right.*

MONIQUE
That tree's not young, is it?

> *As she crosses to place the chair under it, PAULETTE goes back inside rather than follow her.*

It was already there when Simon got married. I didn't know an apple tree could live that long. I think… (Wait a sec…) Is it the same one? I have a picture of me sitting right here. With Pierre. My first husband…? Do you remember Pierre?
(*As she turns around, she notices that PAULETTE isn't there.*)
Paulette?

> *MONIQUE goes back up to the veranda as JOSÉE comes running in from the direction of the driveway.*

JOSÉE
Auntie! Auntie! Here! *(as she hands her the key:)* Thank you.
(*She backs out, heading in the direction she came from.*)
I'm right about what I said! I am!
(*And then, as she moves off and all the way out:*)

If you keep putting things off all the time... I mean fuck... if you never do anything, it'll only get worse.... And then? Then what?

> *MONIQUE puts the key back into her purse and then goes back to sit on the swing again as PAULETTE comes back out with a book, a pack of cigarettes and a lighter. Without a moment's hesitation, she heads right over to her chair under the apple tree.*

PAULETTE
You like the swing, do you?

MONIQUE
D'you?

PAULETTE
I don't trust it. D'you see the rust?

> *MONIQUE looks at the chains that hold the swing as SIMON, LOUISE and ANDRÉ Mathieu return from a tour of the property. We hear them rather than see them at first. They will arrive from the direction of the barn.*

LOUISE   *(off)*
Dad.

SIMON   *(off)*
He's never driven one. He's sixty...?

ANDRÉ   *(off)*
Fifty-seven.

SIMON   *(off)*
He's nearly sixty years old. You'll see. There's nothing to it. Around here, they teach you how to drive one of those things when you're still in diapers.

LOUISE   *(off)*
Dad, I'm definitely not letting the two of you go down there with the tractor.

> *As they arrive on stage, we realize that SIMON is carrying a second sawhorse and LOUISE and ANDRÉ are carrying a piece of plywood for the table. They put these down during the following:*

SIMON
I want to show him. He's interested.

LOUISE
It's an old shack that's falling apart. There's nothing to see.
(to ANDRÉ)
There's nothing to see, Mr. Mathieu.

ANDRÉ *(correcting her)*
André.

SIMON
André, I wouldn't lie to you. It's true, the place…. For someone who doesn't know much about these things…

LOUISE
Dad…

SIMON
For someone who hasn't got any imagination, or…

LOUISE
Dad…

SIMON
Or any kind of flair, you know, for…

LOUISE
Dad…

SIMON
Okay, the place has seen better days. We haven't used it for eight years.

LOUISE
Eight? More like twenty.

SIMON
Lou-Lou…

SIMON shows LOUISE that his water bottle is empty.

MONIQUE *(to LOUISE)*
The sugar shack?

LOUISE
What else.

SIMON
And bring me the key for the tractor.

    LOUISE goes into the house.

MONIQUE *(to LOUISE)*
It's still there?

SIMON
That building's as solid as a rock. It's been there for a hundred years.

PAULETTE
A hundred years?!

SIMON
Almost. Nineteen eighteen. Almost.

PAULETTE
Hasn't been a hundred years. I'm sure of it. My father built it after I was born.

SIMON
There're two copper vats with stamps on them. Nineteen eighteen that's what's written. Those two vats, they're museum pieces.

ANDRÉ
You want to turn it into a museum?

SIMON
A museum? Why would I want to do that? No, no. Production. Production! (We could always set up a little museum beside it, I suppose.) But that'd be a side-line. What I'm talking to you about is "production." I'm talking about "the development of a regional resource."

MONIQUE *(in the direction of the house, without moving)*
Do you need help, Louise?

SIMON
I made a few phone calls, I went and got a few estimates, I talked to a few people. And, I had a few surprises. Good ones and bad ones. More good than bad though.
(LOUISE enters from the house with another bottle of water for SIMON.)
No one takes me seriously. Not yet! But I'm in the process of figuring it all out, and when I do, they'll see my idea is not as crazy

as all that. Next step, we go get ourselves some investors to get the place up and running again.

LOUISE
Watch out, Mr. Mathieu. He's an old smoothie.

ANDRÉ
André.

SIMON
I'm younger than he is!

MONIQUE *(to ANDRÉ)*
Your son hasn't called?

ANDRÉ gestures "no."

LOUISE
I think you should ask him about acid rain, André.

SIMON
You complicate everything!

LOUISE *(to PAULETTE)*
Paulette? A Coke?

SIMON
She complicates everything. You complicate everything.

LOUISE *(to ANDRÉ)*
A beer? Some lemonade?

ANDRÉ Thank you. Uh…?
(to SIMON)
I've read about that… maple trees and acid rain…
(to LOUISE)
Lemonade.
(to SIMON)
It's done a lot of damage.

SIMON
Worse further south. In the States.

LOUISE
Here too.

SIMON
I didn't say it hadn't here.

LOUISE
>Trees died. Production dropped. So did profits. Couldn't make money at it anymore.
>*(to PAULETTE)*
>Paulette?
>*(to SIMON)*
>Never had, really. Even before acid rain.

SIMON
>It was a cottage industry. Around here, that's all it ever was.

LOUISE
>No marketing plan, no distribution network, no… no nothing.
>*(to PAULETTE)*
>A Coke with ice?

SIMON
>But I'll tell you something, it was *darn good* syrup! It was as good as any maple syrup in the whole province of Quebec.

MONIQUE
>Our maple syrup? Never tasted anything like it anywhere.

PAULETTE
>I don't know if I want a Coke.

LOUISE
>Some lemonade, then?

ANDRÉ
>It's a luxury item, in France.

SIMON
>And in Japan…

ANDRÉ
>I read about that.

SIMON
>…gold!

ANDRÉ
>I read that.

SIMON
>Liquid gold!

PAULETTE
> No, a Coke. But with lots of ice.

SIMON
> There's a lot of money to be made with maple syrup. If a fella does it right. A lot of money!

LOUISE
> The only way to make money with that maple bush is if you sell it. (*SIMON makes a face. They've been through this before. But LOUISE goes on for ANDRÉ's sake.*)
> There are thirty-three lots—not small ones, big ones—and at least half are waterfront, on a river you can swim in.

SIMON
> We're not selling the maple bush, Lou-Lou.

LOUISE
> You sell them, lot by lot, or better still, you develop them yourself. Cottages, country homes...

SIMON
> We're too far from the city.

LOUISE
> That's what you said about the golf course. You said the golf course would never get off the ground because of that. And look. It's full. They're expanding next year.

SIMON
> The golf course is one thing; your idea is something else.
> (*to ANDRÉ*)
> But my idea! Wait 'til you see the place.
> (*directed at LOUISE*)
> Lou-Lou, you didn't bring me the key?

LOUISE
> No. I didn't bring you the key.

> > *SIMON starts for the house.*

MONIQUE
> No one's making maple syrup around here anymore?

SIMON
> Not around here.

MONIQUE
It was good.

SIMON
It was superb!

> *SIMON goes into the house. LOUISE follows him.*

LOUISE
Dad! It's out of the question that you go down…. Mum! Mum! Come talk some sense into this husband of yours!

> *ANDRÉ takes his cell phone out of his trouser pocket.*

ANDRÉ
I thought he'd be on death's door the way you talked about him.

MONIQUE
If you'd known him before, you wouldn't say that.

ANDRÉ (*pointing toward the barn, lowering his voice*)
They can actually make a living out of this?

MONIQUE
They do the best they can. They manage.

ANDRÉ
What I saw was pretty run down.
(*looks at his cell phone*)
Ah. Now I know why he hasn't called.

MONIQUE
Your battery?

ANDRÉ
Yeah. They were inducing at two o'clock.
(*looking at his watch*)
Three hours earlier in San Francisco.

> *MONIQUE touches him.*

MONIQUE
You can call your son later. Do you love me?

> *Short pause. Then, softly:*

ANDRÉ
When we go back to the bed and breakfast…

MONIQUE
   Yes?

>   *He whispers in her ear. Short pause. She takes one of his hands and rests it on one of her breasts making sure that PAULETTE can't see them. He starts to feel her up.*

ANDRÉ
   Let's make an excuse and leave early?
   (*She agrees. Smiles. He takes his hand away. Then, he puts his cell phone back in his pocket and starts to move toward the house.*)
   I'm going to go use their phone, I'll leave him / the number here…

MONIQUE
   André, wait.
   (*MONIQUE brings ANDRÉ over to PAULETTE.*)
   Paulette, you haven't met him yet, so I want / to introduce…

PAULETTE
   I know who he is. He's your fiancé. I've heard the whole story.
   (*to ANDRÉ*)
   I know what you're thinking. "She's an ornery old bird." Well, I am!
   (*She laughs out loud. MONIQUE and ANDRÉ laugh too. But politely. During the following, PAULETTE takes a cigarette out of her pack and lights it.*)
   I know all about him. He's a Mathieu. But not one of the Mathieus from around here. Which is just as well because the Mathieus from 'round here are known for only one thing, Mr. Mathieu, there's always at least one of them in prison.
   I can be real ornery.
   (*Same routine with the laughs.*)
   Go get me an ashtray, Monique. Your brother gives me a hard time if I leave my butts all over his lawn.
   (*MONIQUE exits toward the house.*)
   Mr. Mathieu…

ANDRÉ
   André.

PAULETTE
   Mr. Mathieu, I'm an ornery old woman. I was real nice all my life, tried to please everyone, but six months ago something went *crack* in my head, all of sudden, and since that *crack*, I'm ornery. So I've gotta tell you that if I call you Mr. Mathieu instead of André, it's not

because you're from the city or because your trousers are so nicely pressed or because you smell of aftershave that cost you an arm and a leg, it's to annoy you. I'm ornery, ay.

> *She laughs very loudly again. This time ANDRÉ tries even harder to do the same. SIMON comes out of the house with the key.*

SIMON
Know how to use a clutch, André?

ANDRÉ
Oh, it's been years…

SIMON
You can't do much damage to the transmission on a thing like that anyway.

> *MONIQUE arrives with a large black standing ashtray (an antique) and puts it down beside PAULETTE.*

JEANNE *(from inside)*
Simon!

SIMON
Come on, let's get out of here. Come on, come on…

> *LOUISE arrives holding a tray. There are empty glasses on it (for the lemonade) and a tall glass full of Coke for PAULETTE.*

LOUISE
Mum wants to talk to you.

JEANNE *(from inside)*
Simon!

PAULETTE
He's got the key for the tractor.

LOUISE *(toward the house)*
He took the key!

SIMON
André…

LOUISE
Dad, don't do this.

SIMON
We can't go in his car. He'd ruin it.

LOUISE
The radio just said it's thirty-eight degrees…

SIMON
We'll be back in forty minutes? …An hour tops…

LOUISE
They're warning people with heart conditions not / to go outside…

SIMON
I'm not an invalid!

> *JEANNE comes out of the house. She's carrying a man's straw hat with her.*

JEANNE
Simon! No!

SIMON
It's just a little ride on the tractor!

JEANNE
You've done enough for one day and supper's / almost ready… and…

SIMON
I spent my life on a tractor.

JEANNE
It's too hot…

SIMON
You're not going to stop / me from…

JEANNE
And…. Do it for me, okay?… I'll worry. You know me, I'll worry.

> *A short pause.*

SIMON
I wanted to show him the sugar bush.

LOUISE
Gaby can take him down in the truck after supper.

JEANNE
We'll see.
(to SIMON)
Can I have the key back?
(Game: SIMON holds out the key. JEANNE reaches for it. SIMON pulls it away and then laughs.)
Simon...
(SIMON stops laughing, holds the key out to her... same game.)
Simon...

> *SIMON starts again but faster. Then he pretends to throw the key to ANDRÉ.*

SIMON
André! Catch!

> *JEANNE is getting fed up. SIMON continues to clown around but... suddenly, he makes a false move and he falls.*

JEANNE
Simon!

SIMON
It's nothing.

LOUISE
Dad!

SIMON
It's nothing, it's / nothing, nothing.

ANDRÉ
Here, let me help you.

SIMON
No. I'm all right.

LOUISE
Give me your hand.

SIMON
I don't need a hand. I don't need help.
(He gets up, laughing.)
I was acting the fool and the good Lord punished me.

> *Once SIMON is standing:*

JEANNE
　　Let me see you walk to make sure nothing's broken. Did you sprain something?

SIMON
　　I'm fine. Look.

　　　　　SIMON does a little gig.

LOUISE
　　(That's right, go on, fall again…)

JEANNE　*(firmly)*
　　The key.
　　(He hands it to her laughing. She hands him the hat.)
　　And put this on, please.
　　(He takes the hat and looks at it as JEANNE goes back into the house.)
　　It's past five o'clock, by the way.

SIMON
　　What?… Oh. Right. Five o'clock.
　　(A short pause. Then, to MONIQUE as he puts the hat on:)
　　Monique, who does this hat remind you of?
　　(to LOUISE)
　　Louise, can you bring me my pill?
　　(to MONIQUE)
　　Come on, Monique… don't you see it?

　　　　　LOUISE goes back into the house.

MONIQUE
　　Uncle Aurele?

SIMON
　　Yes. Spitting image, eh?

MONIQUE
　　Spitting image.

　　　　　He takes off the hat, looks at it, puts it back on. Short pause. Then, as he goes to sit down on one of the chairs on the veranda:

SIMON
　　Yep. Don't make 'em like that anymore, men like Uncle Aurele. (No, siree.)
　　(Once he's sat down, he takes the hat off again and throws it down on

> *the chair next to him.)*
> (No, siree bob. Not anymore.)
>
> > *He takes a drink from the bottle. A long drink. Uneasy feeling.*

MONIQUE
We should all be wearing something on our heads.

ANDRÉ
Yes.
Yes. Well, tomorrow, on the course, if you aren't wearing something on your head…. Have to. Otherwise… well…

> *Short pause. As ANDRÉ goes to sit on the swing:*

MONIQUE
If it's anything like today, we won't play.

ANDRÉ
We've paid for it, Monique. The green fee's paid for.

MONIQUE
What if it rains?

ANDRÉ
It won't rain.
(pointing to the place on the swing beside him)
Monique.

> *She seems to want to answer back but just at that moment we hear the toot-toots of the horn of the car driving down the concession road out front. Everyone looks far off. SIMON waves his hand.*

MONIQUE
Who's that?

SIMON
No idea. You, Paulette?

PAULETTE *(without looking)*
Simon, I can barely recognize you from where I'm sitting. (So, what's happening down on the road…)

ANDRÉ *(again pointing to the place beside him, more insistent, low)*
Monique…

> *She crosses over, glances quickly at the chains holding it up.*

MONIQUE
Euh… I'm going to see if Jeanne needs me.

> *She goes into the house. A long pause. ANDRÉ swings back and forth. It squeaks.*

SIMON
Golf's supposed to be good for…

> *SIMON touches his head.*

ANDRÉ
It's excellent for the mind. Excellent.

SIMON
Apparently.

ANDRÉ
Excellent.
Three years back, when Lucie died… my wife, Lucie…?

SIMON
Yes…

ANDRÉ
When she died, that's when I realized that golf has helped me grow as a human being.

SIMON
Hm.

ANDRÉ
Mentally.

SIMON
Hm.

ANDRÉ
Mentally. Emotionally. And spiritually.
They're all connected.
It's something you understand, up here, *(He taps his head.)* but when you actually live through it, it's a different thing altogether. Especially when you're getting over the death of a loved one. When you're grieving.
When Lucie passed, we were about to celebrate our thirty-second

wedding anniversary. Thirty-two years, Simon.
If I hadn't had golf...
You don't play, do you?
(*SIMON shakes his head.*)
I'm not sure you can understand me, then.
You see, once I told someone what I just told you, someone who didn't play, who didn't know golf – about Lucie, golf, grieving – and that person... who was someone I loved, someone I thought would understand me... anyway, that person... I don't know whether she didn't want to understand, but she didn't understand that going out and hitting a few balls that morning—Lucie died at dawn—that hitting a few balls, playing eighteen holes that Wednesday morning after leaving the hospital, right after she passed away, did me a great deal of good.
To my soul.
I even knocked two points off my handicap.
(*ANDRÉ's attention is drawn to something happening over by the cars.*)
It was my daughter... I won't hide it from you... my daughter, Maude. According to her, (someone's here) in her opinion, I showed a lack of respect toward her mother.
(*We hear a car horn. It's important to note that the sound of this horn in no way resembles the sound of the horn of the car that drives by on the concession road. This is the family pick-up truck and the sound comes from the area where the cars are parked.*)
She still holds it against me. I don't know. Maybe someone who doesn't know golf just can't understand. But to go out on a golf course, play eighteen holes, was a natural thing for me to do. It was...

    LOUISE enters from the house.

SIMON (*to LOUISE*)
 It's Gaby.

LOUISE
 Yes.
 (*We hear the sound of a horn again. This time, from another car.*)
 He's not alone.

    LOUISE gives SIMON his pill.

SIMON *(about the pill, annoyed)*
This isn't the right one! It's the pink one at five o'clock!

LOUISE *(angry)*
Don't talk to me like that! I'm not your servant!
(She takes the pill from him and turns and goes back into the house.)
And put your hat back on!

> Pause.

SIMON
It's lousy being sick, André. Really lousy. Keep in shape with that golf of yours. It's a good thing.

GABRIEL *(off)*
Simon! Christ, Simon! Wait 'til you see this!
(GABRIEL enters holding a gunny bag. One of his hands is in the bag. He's very excited.)
You've never seen anything like it. Christ!
(to ANDRÉ)
Sorry. I'm sorry. I don't usually use that kind of language.
(to SIMON)
C'here, Simon. Come see.

SIMON
What is it?

GABRIEL
I don't want to do it on the veranda.
(SIMON stays seated, but ANDRÉ comes closer.)
Mr. Mathieu?

ANDRÉ
André.

GABRIEL
Sorry. Really, I don't usually swear like that. Right, Paulette? It's true, eh? I'm not like that. But this…
(the bag moves)
Christ!

SIMON
Those your two buddies in the other car?

GABRIEL
Yep. They're waitin' for me. I gotta give it back to 'em. Jack—he's the

one who caught it—Jack wants to take it to Paquin…
(to ANDRÉ)
The vet. If anyone should see this, it's Paquin.

SIMON
What do you / want to show…

GABRIEL *(pointing to the sack)*
It's a snake. Well a garter snake…
(ANDRÉ freezes.)
But goddam it! It's seven / feet long at least…

ANDRÉ
Dead?

GABRIEL
No, no. Alive. Very much alive.

PAULETTE *(very interested)*
Let me see.

SIMON
Can't be seven feet. Impossible.

GABRIEL
I'm tellin' you. It's a freak of nature.

SIMON
Seven feet? Impossible!

GABRIEL
Maybe more! Maybe eight!

SIMON
Impossible! There aren't any garter snakes around here seven feet long!

GABRIEL
Louise! Bring me the old measuring sticks that are behind the kitchen door!

PAULETTE
Show me.

MONIQUE is at the door. She comes out.

MONIQUE
What is it? What's / happening?

GABRIEL takes the head of the snake out of the bag.

SIMON
A snake. Gaby / brought it…

She hurries back inside.

MONIQUE
Oh! I hate those things! What's he doing with that? Jeanne!

MONIQUE goes to get JEANNE in the house.

SIMON *(with a smile)*
Now my sister's getting all worked up.

MONIQUE *(from inside)*
Jeanne!

PAULETTE
Take the whole thing out! / Take it out! Come on, take it out!

SIMON *(toward the house)*
You grew up in the country, Monique! For God's sake, you've seen a garter snake before.
God's sake!

ANDRÉ
You got a good hold on it?

GABRIEL
Yeah, yeah…
(GABRIEL holds the snake's head outside the bag for PAULETTE's sake all through the following.)
She's a beauty, eh?

PAULETTE
You going to kill it?

GABRIEL
Course not!
(to SIMON)
Methot spotted it. It was him / while he was…

SIMON
Methot? What was he doing there?

GABRIEL
I'll tell you about that. Wait.

PAULETTE
You should kill it. You should / cut its head off.

GABRIEL *(ignoring PAULETTE)*
So anyway, Methot's right there, you know, talking to me, he's talking to me, ya know…

SIMON
What about?

GABRIEL
About the fields he's supposed to be renting, okay? So he's there / talking to me…

SIMON
What do you mean "supposed"? It's a done deal!

GABRIEL
I know. Simon, I know!
(From now on GABRIEL talks to ANDRÉ rather than SIMON. ANDRÉ is keeping his distance.)
Anyway, he's talking to me when, suddenly, he looks in the ditch 'cause something caught his eye, okay?…

PAULETTE
My father liked to kill them.

GABRIEL
And it's this thing here, eating a toad. Not a little toad either! A big huge one! You should see the jaws on this thing when they're open!

> *JEANNE arrives and stands in the doorway. She talks through the screen door.*

PAULETTE
Papa called them "foul and loathsome creatures." / Yeah. That was it. "Foul and loathsome creatures."

GABRIEL
We caught it 'cause it was eating. / It wouldn't let go of the toad.

> *Through this next section three conversations are going on: GABRIEL and ANDRÉ, SIMON and JEANNE on the veranda, and finally, PAULETTE talking to the snake.*

GABRIEL
The snake wanted to get away but it didn't want to drop the toad.

But the toad was slowing it down. It was like it didn't know what it wanted most... or something like that. So finally, it was easy enough to catch it 'cause as long as it had the toad in its mouth, eh?, well it couldn't bite or anything, 'cause, you know, they say garter·snakes don't bite, and usually, sure, a garter snake won't bite you. They never bite. But you know, a big one like this! I don't know. It's hard to believe it wouldn't bite to defend itself.

JEANNE
Why did he bring a snake back here?

SIMON
It's seven feet long, apparently.

PAULETTE *(bringing her hand close to the snake's jaws)*
Come on, stick out your tongue.

JEANNE
Impossible.

SIMON
I know.

PAULETTE
Stick it out for me.

JEANNE
Garter snakes can't be seven / feet long.

SIMON
I know. He says it's a "freak of nature."

JEANNE *(toward the house)*
Louise!

MONIQUE *(from inside)*
Is it still there?

JEANNE *(toward the house)*
Stay inside. *(louder)* Louise!

PAULETTE
Oh! It touched me!
(GABRIEL stops telling ANDRÉ the snake story.)
Did you see it?

GABRIEL
Did it stick out its tongue?

PAULETTE
    Yes, its tongue, its little forked tongue...
    (to ANDRÉ)
    Come see, come see...

ANDRÉ
    Its tongue. Yes. I saw...

        LOUISE comes out of the house, hands her father a bottle of pills, but talks to GABRIEL.

LOUISE
    Gaby, do you really have a snake in that bag?

GABRIEL
    Look!

        GABRIEL starts to take the snake out of the bag. ANDRÉ backs up.

LOUISE
    No, no, not here!

PAULETTE
    Take the whole thing out!

LOUISE
    Not here! My aunt's having a conniption fit.

GABRIEL
    Really?

LOUISE
    Yes, really. Yes.

        Short pause.

GABRIEL
    Sorry.
    (GABRIEL puts the snake back in the bag. Then, loudly, in MONIQUE's direction.)
    Monique! I'm sorry.
    (to the others)
    I wanted to show it to you. Have to give it back to Jack anyway.
    (toward the house)
    Monique! I'm sorry. I'm going now.

LOUISE
Wait. Let me see.

> *LOUISE crosses to GABRIEL who takes the snake's head out of the bag for her to see.*

GABRIEL
Beautiful, eh?
(*A long enough pause. They're all fascinated by the snake. And then, quickly, practically in a whisper.*)
Catching a snake brings luck.

LOUISE
Who told you that?

GABRIEL
Isn't that what they say?

ANDRÉ
I think it varies from one culture to another, one country to another...

LOUISE
Here?

ANDRÉ
Here... I don't know about here.

GABRIEL
Paulette?

PAULETTE
I don't remember. I know that Papa used to kill them by cutting off their heads. But catching them and killing them are two different things.

GABRIEL
Seems to me I always heard it was lucky?

> *Pause.*

MONIQUE (*from inside*)
Can I come out?

GABRIEL (*toward the house*)
I'm sorry, Monique. I didn't think. I'm going now.

> GABRIEL *puts the snake back in the bag and starts to exit.*

SIMON
Gaby! Use some baling twine to measure it. You got any baling twine in the truck?

GABRIEL
Okay, I'll see…

SIMON
You take the twine / and you use it to…

GABRIEL
It's okay. That's what I'll do.

SIMON
And I want to know what Methot said!
(to ANDRÉ)
Go on, André, if you want to see it.

LOUISE
Go on, they'll show it to you.

ANDRÉ
Yes.
(GABRIEL exits. Short pause. Then, ANDRÉ follows heading off in the direction of the cars.)
Yes.

> LOUISE *goes back into the house.* SIMON *takes his pill, drinks from the bottle of water, and then, goes over to the door.*

SIMON
You can come out now, Monique!

MONIQUE *(from inside)*
You sure?

SIMON
Yes, come on out.

> MONIQUE *enters as he goes into the house.*

MONIQUE
I hate those things.

> MONIQUE *sighs. She goes and gets the travel brochure she left on the swing. Is about to sit down but changes her mind and stays standing.*

PAULETTE
They're measuring it.

MONIQUE
Yeah.

> *Short pause. Then, as though attracted despite herself, she crosses down to where PAULETTE is sitting muttering as she goes "I hate those things, oh, I hate them so much, I hate them, I hate them, I hate them." As the two women talk, they stare at the area where the cars are parked.*

I hate them so much.

PAULETTE
Little critters don't eat big ones, Monique.

MONIQUE
Right.

> *Short pause.*

PAULETTE
You want to go see it?

MONIQUE
See the snake?! Course not!

> *Short pause. Then, showing MONIQUE her finger.*

PAULETTE
It touched me.
(MONIQUE shivers with disgust.)
With its tongue.
(Same reaction from MONIQUE, but not quite as pronounced this time.)
A caress. Yes. You might say it was a tiny, gentle caress.
(Again the same reaction of disgust from MONIQUE. Even less pronounced this time.)
You want to go, don't you?

MONIQUE
Of course I don't!

(She hands her the brochure while still staring off to where the snake is.)
Here. That's Alaska.
(PAULETTE starts reading.)
Where I'm going on my honeymoon. The boat on the cover, that's our boat. It looks really small up against the mountains, but there are two swimming pools on that boat. Two pools, a movie theatre, three maybe four restaurants, a casino, a ballroom, a bowling alley, can't remember how many elevators, a beauty parlour, mini-golf, a chapel.... There's everything on there.
You wouldn't think it to look at the picture. In the picture, it looks like a toy.
Have you ever wanted to go to Alaska?

PAULETTE
Never.

MONIQUE
Me neither. Doesn't interest me. Not in the least. It's never interested me. I don't know why I said yes.
I was twenty-five years old when I left my first husband, and I left him because he was jealous, he wouldn't let me live. I spent the next thirty years of my life doing everything on my own. Everything for myself. And now, I'm going on a cruise to Alaska—a place that absolutely doesn't interest me—with a man I met a year and a half ago at a New Year's Eve party I didn't really want to go to. A man who tells me he likes a woman who wears bracelets, so he buys me some... and...
I've never worn bracelets.
If the woman I was ten years ago—even five years ago—could see me today, she wouldn't recognize me. She would've said "no" to him, but I said "Alaska? Why not?"

PAULETTE
Six.
(MONIQUE looks perplexed.)
There are six restaurants. Twelve elevators.

SIMON enters from the house.

SIMON
Monique, Jeanne just told me she agreed to go visit you next week?

> *She nods. Then she crosses to join him and speaks softly so that neither PAULETTE nor JEANNE can hear them.*

MONIQUE
You were right though. I had to insist.

SIMON
I knew she wouldn't want to. Did she talk to you about / what I told you?

> *But they're interrupted by PAULETTE, who's looking in the direction of the cars again...*

PAULETTE
What are they doing? Simon, can you see what they're doing?

> *...and by ANDRÉ who enters quickly from that direction.*

MONIQUE
What's happening, André?

ANDRÉ
It got away! The snake got away!

> *MONIQUE lets out a cry of disgust. PAULETTE smiles.*

MONIQUE
Oh! Ohohoh...
(as she heads back toward the house)
(Damn it damn it damn it!) I hate those things!

SIMON
Little critters don't eat / big ones, Monique.

MONIQUE
...eat big ones. Heard it before.

SIMON
Well if you've heard it...

MONIQUE
That's enough out of you, little brother! You've always loved to laugh at me. Ever since we were kids.
(She's reached the door, but turns around before going in.)
André, are you going back to help them catch it?

ANDRÉ
   Well… there's already three of them… I don't think / that…

MONIQUE
   All right then, call your son.
   (as she enters)
   Jeanne? André wants to call his son, can he use your telephone?

SIMON
   Geez, Monique, you going to spend the whole visit in the house because of a garter snake?

>   *MONIQUE comes back to the screen door but stays inside.*

MONIQUE   *(from inside)*
   I've got only one thing to say to you, Simon. Like in that American movie? "What part of 'go fuck yourself' don't you understand?"

ANDRÉ
   Monique!

MONIQUE
   And, the same goes for you, if you side with him!

SIMON   *(laughing)*
   Learning a thing or two you didn't know about your future wife, eh André!?
   (He spots GABRIEL coming back from the direction of the cars.)
   So?

GABRIEL
   Gone. When those things take off, well… eh Mr. Mathieu?

PAULETTE   *(correcting him)*
   André.

GABRIEL
   What?

ANDRÉ
   It was very impressive, yes.

GABRIEL
   It took off… ohohoh yeah!

>   *GABRIEL helps himself to a large glass of lemonade and downs it in one go. ANDRÉ will do the same.*

SIMON
What direction?

GABRIEL
Over to the right. Toward the ditch.

SIMON
They'll never find it.

GABRIEL
That's what I told them. They won't look long.

SIMON *(to ANDRÉ)*
It wasn't seven feet long, was it?

ANDRÉ
Well... it wasn't small let me tell you.

> *We hear a car horn tooting. LOUISE comes out of the house.*

GABRIEL
Is that Josée?

> *A few more toots. More insistent this time.*

SIMON
What's she getting worked up about?

GABRIEL
She must want the guys to leave so she can park.

> *LOUISE goes over to the two sawhorses.*

LOUISE
Someone want to give me a hand?

> *GABRIEL comes over and the two of them put up the table during the following. The next few lines are spoken softly at the same time as JEANNE and MONIQUE enter.*

GABRIEL
We lost the snake.

LOUISE
Oh.
(reacting to the smell)
You smell. Whew! / You really stink.

GABRIEL
Yeah, but… what d'ya expect?

LOUISE
I know.

GABRIEL
I'll go take a shower right away. (I stink, I stink…)

> *JEANNE has entered. She heads straight over to her mother. She hands her a pill which PAULETTE will swallow with some Coke. PAULETTE will nod off after that. MONIQUE has followed JEANNE outside. She has a cordless phone in her hand and she hands it to ANDRÉ while talking to her brother.*

MONIQUE
Simon, about the wedding…? / About after…?

JEANNE
Monique, that's all settled.

MONIQUE
Seems to me that it would be so much easier if you stayed over. Less tiring for Paulette, too.

JEANNE
It's settled.

MONIQUE
Yes, but things have changed.

JEANNE
It's settled. We made a decision.

ANDRÉ
You're talking about the hotel room?

LOUISE
That was settled. After the reception, we're coming straight back here.

> *During what follows, ANDRÉ will dial a number a few times before getting through. He's making a call to California with his calling card.*

ANDRÉ
Yes, but I have news about the room.

MONIQUE *(to ANDRÉ)*
Did they catch the snake?
(ANDRÉ shakes his head "no." MONIQUE shudders in disgust.)
(Oh! Shit…)

SIMON
We talked it over, but…

LOUISE
But it's "no."

ANDRÉ
Except now, I've got some good news.

LOUISE *(to SIMON, firmly almost rudely)*
It's "no."

> *LOUISE goes back into the house. GABRIEL pours himself some more lemonade. He'll finish the pitcher.*

JEANNE
It's not the price or / the money or…

MONIQUE
We know that. We never thought it was.

ANDRÉ
The news is we have a suite—not a room, a suite—we got it for nothing. It's included.

MONIQUE
It comes with. With the rental of the hall.

ANDRÉ
It's included. I didn't know that. When I went there to pay for the rental, they showed it to me.

SIMON
But you're still paying for it.

ANDRÉ
No, it's included. It's not more expensive with it, it's not less expensive without it. There's one price. Non-negotiable.

MONIQUE
It's lovely, apparently. Huge. Two rooms. You wouldn't be cramped.

ANDRÉ
There are two double beds in the bedroom and a queen-size pull-out couch in the living room. There's even two televisions. One... *(into the telephone)* Yes. Michel?

MONIQUE
One in the bedroom. One in the living room.

ANDRÉ *(on the telephone)*
Oh. Hi.
(to MONIQUE)
It's Trish's mother.
(on the phone)
It's André.

> *ANDRÉ moves off a little and his conversation on the phone continues parallel to the rest of the dialogue.*

SIMON
Oh yeah...

ANDRÉ *(on the phone)*
Yes. From the Great White North. Yes.

JEANNE
Isn't it meant for the bride and groom? For their wedding night?

MONIQUE
André's house is ten minutes away.

ANDRÉ *(on the phone)*
How's everything going at the hospital? Good?

JEANNE
But on your wedding night, like that, seems to me / it'd be nice to have a hotel room. To go to sleep knowing you don't have to make the bed in the morning, and you can order breakfast without getting up...

ANDRÉ *(on the phone)*
I'm going to give you a number where he can reach me when the baby's born, okay?

MONIQUE
We leave on a two-week trip at the crack of dawn the next morning.

ANDRÉ *(on the phone)*
You have it?

JEANNE
We wouldn't want to take anything away from you.

ANDRÉ *(on the phone)*
Right. Call display. Right.

MONIQUE
You're not taking anything away from us. We won't use it!

ANDRÉ *(on the phone)*
Yes, that's it. That's the number.

SIMON
Thank you, it's very nice of you, but it's true that we've / already settled it. Right?

MONIQUE
André doesn't want to leave it empty.

ANDRÉ *(on the phone)*
Yes, well, it's hot here too.

GABRIEL
Can we say we'll think about it? Can we say that?

ANDRÉ *(on the phone)*
I'll be there next week.

GABRIEL
We'll think about it. Think, talk. We'll give you an answer this week. Okay?

ANDRÉ *(on the phone)*
Okay.

MONIQUE
Okay.

ANDRÉ *(on the phone)*
Okay.

JEANNE *(to GABRIEL)*
I need you to bring out the chairs.

> *ANDRÉ hangs up. GABRIEL goes into the house. JOSÉE hurries in from the direction of the cars. She's carrying*

> *a grocery bag containing two baskets of raspberries, her mother's purse, and her waitress uniform which she picked up at the dry cleaners. JEANNE who was following GABRIEL into the house, stops when she hears:*

JOSÉE
> Grandma!

MONIQUE
> Jeanne and Simon are going to think about it.
> (*Short pause. ANDRÉ looks perplexed.*)
> The suite. They're going to think about it.

ANDRÉ
> Oh! Okay.

> *JOSÉE holds up the grocery bag as she moves toward JEANNE.*

JEANNE
> How much do I owe you?

JOSÉE
> Seven.

JEANNE (*as she takes the bag from JOSÉE*)
> You didn't pay more than three dollars!? At / the Rioux...

JOSÉE
> You wanted them? Okay, here. I told you I wouldn't go to the Rioux!

MONIQUE (*to JOSÉE*)
> Did they leave with the snake?
> (*JOSÉE shakes her head. MONIQUE shudders with disgust.*)
> (Oh! Shit...)

> *As she enters the house, JOSÉE meets her father coming out carrying two chairs.*

GABRIEL
> Grab two and bring 'em out, okay.

JOSÉE
> No time. I'm taking a shower and leaving.

> *GABRIEL puts the chairs down and then starts to go back into the house, but SIMON stops him.*

SIMON
Gab! I want to know... Methot? What did he want?

JEANNE *(going into the house)*
We've got guests, no business.

    Once JEANNE is inside.

GABRIEL
It's the Swiss guy.

SIMON
Bush?

GABRIEL
Bausch, yeah. The Swiss guy offered to lease him pasture for less.

SIMON
We had an understanding. We shook hands on it.

GABRIEL
Hey Simon, I know. He says he didn't sign anything, so...

SIMON
Goddam Bush!

GABRIEL *(as he enters the house)*
Bausch.

SIMON
Goddam Methot!

MONIQUE
Is that Real?

SIMON
His son.

JEANNE *(from inside)*
Monique!

SIMON
A handshake means nothing to that guy. (Doesn't mean a thing to him.)

MONIQUE *(as she goes into the house)*
André, go get the cooler in the car.

    SIMON goes to the car with ANDRÉ.

SIMON *(to ANDRÉ)*
These days, André, a handshake doesn't mean a thing. Has no value. None! None at all!

ANDRÉ
When we were young…

SIMON
When we were young…!

ANDRÉ
It wasn't the same.

SIMON
When we were young… I'm not saying there weren't assholes around. There were. Maybe even as many as today. Except back then, an asshole was an asshole and we weren't afraid to say it or to think it. Today…
If I tell some people what Methot just did to me? You think they'll say he's an asshole? No. They'll tell me I'm blowing the whole thing out of proportion, that he's just a guy who's got a good head for business. Christ! A good head for business!

ANDRÉ
What's it about exactly? The two fields…? I didn't / quite understand what…

SIMON
It's nothing. It's a little…. It's nothing.

> *He continues as they exit. GABRIEL enters with two chairs and holds the door open for LOUISE who's following him with a tablecloth and the dinner plates in her hands. Their conversation is fast and low.*

But it's an example, damn it! An example of everything that's going wrong. IN. THE. WORLD. TODAY, André. Do you understand what I'm saying?

GABRIEL
Louise… I think it would make them happy. Aunt Monique and her Mr. Mathieu.

LOUISE
Oh, yes?

GABRIEL
You can sleep in the bedroom with your parents if you want.

LOUISE
That's not it.

GABRIEL
I can take the sofa.

LOUISE
That's not it.

GABRIEL
It's for your parents too. When's the last time they got to spend a night in a big hotel? A little luxury, y'know…?

LOUISE
It's me. That's it, isn't it.

GABRIEL
We could make an effort. Do it for them, make them happy.

LOUISE
(*I* could make an effort, you mean.)

GABRIEL
One night together…

LOUISE
(It's me.) It's always me!

> Pause. PAULETTE snores.

GABRIEL
Okay. All right. Let's drop it.

LOUISE
(The *bitch*. The shit-disturber.)

GABRIEL
I've dropped it. Okay.

LOUISE
(Never happy.)

GABRIEL
I've dropped it.

LOUISE
   Thank you.

>   *Short pause.*

GABRIEL
   I think your aunt knows.
   I think your mother told her all about it.
   I'm telling you so you know.
   I don't want you to think I'm the one / who complained…

LOUISE
   I saw him again.
   (*The news hits GABRIEL hard. Silence. Then, quickly…*)
   I saw him. I told you I wouldn't see him again, but I did.

>   *Short pause. PAULETTE wakes up with a start muttering "Did you hear it? Eh?"*

>   *LOUISE ignores her and continues to put the tablecloth on the table. JEANNE comes out of the house with another tablecloth. GABRIEL goes back inside during the following.*

JEANNE (*seeing the tablecloth LOUISE is putting on the table*)
   Oh!

LOUISE
   You want to use that one?

JEANNE
   You like the yellow one better? It's true, it's more "summery."

LOUISE
   You decide.

JEANNE
   I thought the white one. You know, white… wedding…

LOUISE
   They're your guests.

JEANNE
   The yellow one's pretty.

LOUISE
   But if you want the white one, we'll use / the white one.

JEANNE
　Oh! leave it, you've already got the yellow one on…

LOUISE
　It's nothing, Mum. We can change it if you want to.

PAULETTE
　We're eating outside?

JEANNE
　It's too hot in the house. With the oven on and everything.

PAULETTE
　What's in the oven?

JEANNE
　A pork roast.
　(LOUISE starts to take the yellow tablecloth off the table.)
　No. Leave the yellow one. We'll use the yellow one.

PAULETTE
　We're eating pork? I can't eat pork. Not today.

LOUISE
　Mum, if you like the white one better…

JEANNE
　What do *you* think?

PAULETTE
　I know what I'd like, an omelette!

LOUISE　*(pointing to the tablecloth in JEANNE's hands)*
　Gimme. Gimme that one.

PAULETTE
　An omelette made with fresh eggs.

LOUISE
　You decide, Mum, and stop…

PAULETTE
　Louise, would you make me an omelette?

LOUISE
　If you want, sure. An omelette? Okay.
　(to JEANNE)
　Gimme.

JEANNE
Forget it. The yellow one's just fine.

> *PAULETTE gets up. During the following, she goes up onto the veranda, takes off her shoes and puts on a pair of rubber boots that are sitting there. LOUISE starts to put the yellow tablecloth on the table. Then, reacting to JEANNE who hasn't moved:*

LOUISE
What?
(short pause)
Are you going to try to make me change my mind about the room too...?

JEANNE
It's not for me, it's for your father. (I think I prefer the white one.)

> *While LOUISE and JEANNE take the yellow tablecloth off the table and replace it with the white one, we hear the beginnings of the conversation (offstage) between SIMON and ANDRÉ who are coming back from the car with the cooler. Once the white cloth is on the table, LOUISE will go back into the house. Then, JEANNE will follow taking the dinner plates with her.*

SIMON   *(off)*
A man's word, well, it's the basis. The basis of everything.

ANDRÉ   *(off)*
That's the way things work now, Simon.

SIMON   *(off)*
A handshake...

ANDRÉ   *(off)*
You've got to be careful.

SIMON   *(off)*
A handshake. If you can't have a minimum amount of trust...

ANDRÉ   *(off)*
You've got to take precautions though.

> *The two men enter.*

SIMON
Yes, but when... when that minimum isn't there...!

ANDRÉ
I'm not disagreeing with you.

SIMON
Then it's a free-for-all, anything goes. And, sooner or later, André....
Sooner or later...

ANDRÉ
I'm saying you're right.

SIMON
...it's not just you who's in trouble, it's everybody!

ANDRÉ
Yes.

SIMON
If you accept that a man's word isn't worth anything, if you accept that, then sooner or later...
(They put the cooler down near the table.)
Sooner or later...

   SIMON drinks from his bottle.

ANDRÉ
Sooner or later, it's chaos.

   MONIQUE enters with yellow napkins. She starts to put them on the table.

MONIQUE *(in a loud voice, toward the house)*
Champagne's here! Everybody outside!

   JEANNE enters with blue napkins. She's about to react to the yellow napkins but notices PAULETTE.

JEANNE *(to PAULETTE)*
Mother? Where are you going?

PAULETTE
To the henhouse. I want some eggs.

JEANNE
We have some.

PAULETTE
I need the exercise. It'll do me good.

SIMON
What'll you do if you run into Gaby's seven-foot snake, Paulette?

PAULETTE
I'll ask Monique to come and save me.

> *Everyone laughs. JEANNE wants to stop her mother from going but is interrupted by JOSÉE who enters in a hurry talking to her. JOSÉE is wearing her waitress's uniform (black trousers, white shirt with a starched collar and a bow tie). She's also done her hair. She sits down and puts on her socks and her black shoes during the following.*

JOSÉE
The extension number of the restaurant at the golf course is on the table in the hall. If Montreal calls, tell them I'll call them right back. Then you phone me over there. Mr. Dupras knows all about it. He'll come get me.

JEANNE
Today's not the day you're supposed to hear.

JOSÉE
Monday. Monday at the latest. But they said they might call over the weekend.

ANDRÉ *(as he takes a bottle of champagne out of the cooler)*
Hear about what?

MONIQUE *(about the uniform)*
Oh, chic!

JOSÉE
Hot more like. *(to JEANNE)* You haven't told him?!

JEANNE *(to MONIQUE)*
The golf club is very chic. Wait 'til you see it.

MONIQUE
Isn't it air conditioned?

JOSÉE
Yeah, but it's still hot. *(to JEANNE)* No one told him?!

> JEANNE *goes back into the house with the yellow napkins. She meets LOUISE on her way out with different dinner plates. MONIQUE takes a "ring" of shrimp out of the cooler.*

MONIQUE
Look, Josée, I remembered. I brought shrimp for you.

JOSÉE
You haven't explained to him?!

LOUISE
Explained what?

JOSÉE
That is so typical! What's going on in my life isn't important!

MONIQUE *(to ANDRÉ)*
Josée's a finalist in a contest.
(Pop! The champagne cork pops. To LOUISE in a whisper:)
The glasses.

JOSÉE
What's happening to me, what could be happening to me...

> JOSÉE *continues even after LOUISE has gone back into the house.*

MONIQUE *(noticing that PAULETTE is heading in the direction of the barn)*
Paulette, we're going to make a toast!

PAULETTE
Save some for me.

JOSÉE
...if it's not about this place... if it's not about cows, pigs, chickens or corn!

SIMON
The cows and the corn are going to pay to send you to school in the city, young lady. Don't forget that.

JOSÉE *(as she eats a shrimp)*
More like the houses Mum sells are paying, Grandad.
(to MONIQUE)
Mmm. These are good.

MONIQUE
Geez, do you always get this worked up?

JOSÉE
I'm nineteen years old. If I don't get worked up, no one pays attention to me.

> *GABRIEL enters from the house with a beer in his hand. LOUISE follows him out with the glasses.*

LOUISE
You didn't take a shower?

JOSÉE
Am I the only one who thinks this isn't normal?! This isn't normal! It's not! No one's asked me for details! No one's asked me a single question! About my hopes? My dreams?

> *JEANNE arrives with her hands full of glasses.*

JEANNE
Gaby, the bathroom's free.

GABRIEL
I'm not the one who's dirty. *(to LOUISE)* I smell of sweat not sex.

JOSÉE
No one wants to know what I want to do with my life!? Don't forget…

JEANNE *(lowering her voice, but firm)*
We have guests.

JOSÉE
I'm the future!

> *JOSÉE exits.*

LOUISE *(as JOSÉE exits)*
You can go on without me.

JEANNE *(firm, still in a low voice)*
We have guests.

> *Short pause. MONIQUE has heard the previous exchange, but continues smiling.*

MONIQUE
Is everyone here?

LOUISE
You go on without me. *(to GABRIEL)* Did you understand what I said? Did you? / Did you hear me?

JEANNE
We have guests. If you two have to talk, do it elsewhere. Your bedroom. Or go for a walk.

LOUISE *(to GABRIEL)*
Did you hear me?

JEANNE
CONTROL YOURSELF!

LOUISE
Yes, okay, yes…

MONIQUE
André would like to say a few words.

LOUISE
No!

LOUISE grabs the cordless phone and punches in a number. She doesn't move away but stays where she is so that everyone can hear.

JEANNE
Simon…

LOUISE *(on the telephone)*
It's me.

JEANNE
Simon…

LOUISE *(on the telephone)*
Yes. D'you want to see me?
I couldn't, but now I can. I want you to come and get me.

JEANNE
Simon…

LOUISE *(on the phone)*
At home, yes… no, no. Everyone's here. Everyone. We'll talk about it later, okay?
No, right away, I don't want to wait.

I can't. It has to be now, right away. Are you coming?
Are you?

>LOUISE *hangs up.*
>
>*A long pause.*
>
>*Then she leaves the table and goes into the house.*

GABRIEL
I have rights.
I've been here twenty-one years next month.
I've never counted my hours. I've never complained when it came to the work that had to be done. You've never heard me whine. Never. Or find excuses to put off until tomorrow what we agreed had to be done that day.
And, I never took a day off work. Never took sick leave 'cause I was never sick. I'm never sick. Which means it's seven out of seven, and ten, twelve, often fourteen hours straight, and I've done sixteen and eighteen-hour days when the rain threatened to ruin everything we'd just harvested 'cause we listened to the girl from Environment Canada...
R'member last September?
(SIMON nods.)
You never heard me complain.
You never heard me talk about what's "owed" me, or say "I'll write that down in my little notebook" like the Rioux boys do with their father. It's a running gag over there.... To make the old man mad...?

JEANNE
They're just kidding.

GABRIEL
I know. I know that. And jokes are all right. But the reason I'm saying this is for some people that's how it works. I'm talking about counting the hours. Because when you do, when you add them up, then at least that's clear. When the rest isn't.
Anymore.
I've never wanted to talk about all this. As far as I was concerned, there was never any question of setting it down in writing in front of a lawyer. Even when you made those arrangements after Simon's accident.

JEANNE
You didn't even want to come in with us.

GABRIEL *(to JEANNE)*
I arrived here with a tool chest, two suitcases of clothes and my old beat-up Plymouth, as far as I'm concerned, it's between you and your legal "survivor."
It's your land, your place. Paulette's, yours…
(to SIMON)
I'm like you, Simon. I'm in the same boat. The only thing you ever signed was the marriage register when you got married. The licence, the register…. But my signature is there! Yours too, Simon! And so are all of yours!
I don't know the law, but in the eyes of the law, well, that counts for somethin'.
I didn't meddle in your business at the notary's, but I did talk to a lawyer. And, he says, it's clear. Clear.
Because she's the one talking about leaving. Not me. It's not me who's walking out. That's gonna count in court. It's gonna count a lot as a matter of fact.

SIMON
We're not in court yet.

GABRIEL
Somebody's gonna pay me back. I'm not leaving here without getting paid back for those twenty-one years. And that's the truth of it.

SIMON
We're not in court and no one's said you have to leave.

GABRIEL
I've got rights.

SIMON
Course you do.

GABRIEL
If she thinks I'm just gonna leave. Pack my bags. Take my tool chest, my clothes, disappear…
(LOUISE enters from the house with a small overnight suitcase.)
I'm an honest man but if your… if that son-of-a-bitch comes up here, the twenty-two's in the truck and I'll use it if I have to.

LOUISE
Don't say that.

GABRIEL
I know how.

SIMON
Don't say things you might regret.

MONIQUE *(wanting to leave)*
André...

ANDRÉ agrees.

LOUISE
I'll wait for him down by the road.

GABRIEL
You'd better.
(LOUISE stares at him)
What?

A short pause.

LOUISE *(in a more conciliatory tone)*
Let's take three days. Without seeing each other. Without talking. After that we'll see what we'll do.

She leaves carrying the suitcase heading in the direction of the cars.

GABRIEL
I've got rights!

MONIQUE
André, we should leave them to...

GABRIEL
Jesus Christ... *(to ANDRÉ)* Sorry.

ANDRÉ
No. You don't have to... it's normal.
I want to...
I want you to know that.... Listen... (this might come out all wrong...) I hope you'll forgive me if I don't say this right...
But this happens to everyone. Every family.
It's never a "pleasant" situation, never...

MONIQUE
Never.

ANDRÉ
My daughter's divorced. It was very ugly. There were young children involved. My grandsons.

MONIQUE
Six and eight when it happened.

ANDRÉ *(to GABRIEL)*
At least, yours is… well, yours is a lovely young girl… a young woman even… and she's already left home or is about to.

MONIQUE
It's easier.

ANDRÉ
It's easier. Maybe not any less painful but…

MONIQUE
It's easier when you don't have to figure out who gets the kids.

ANDRÉ
It was very ugly between my daughter, Maude, and her husband. Lots of bad blood. Got very emotional.

MONIQUE realizes that no one's listening to him.

MONIQUE
André…

ANDRÉ
I wasn't able to follow it all that closely. Under the circumstances. You see, my daughter and I, since her mother passed on, we…

MONIQUE
André…!

ANDRÉ
At any rate…
It's very difficult. With or without children. A trial. A major one. But you get through it. And sometimes it's for the better. Often for the better. Because when you think about it…

MONIQUE *(interrupting him but she doesn't move)*
We're going to leave you.
I want to go, André.

ANDRÉ
Yes.
We're going now.

GABRIEL
I'm gonna smash something. I think I'm gonna smash something.

SIMON
What you need is a good stiff drink. Jeanne, go get the bottle of brandy.

ANDRÉ *(looking in the direction of the cars)*
You have to move your truck.

SIMON
Jeanne.

JEANNE
I'm ashamed. For my daughter.

ANDRÉ
Oh please… it's not…

JEANNE
I want to say it. I want to speak. And I want you to hear me say it.

SIMON
Jeanne.

JEANNE
I'm ashamed. Maybe these things happen, like you said. But still, there's right and wrong. I want you to hear me say it.

GABRIEL
(Yeah…)

JEANNE
There's wrong. There's right.

GABRIEL
(Wrong, yeah…)

JEANNE
And what she's doing, is wrong. What she's doing to him, is wrong. *(She picks up the telephone and heads for the house. As she goes:)*
There I said it. I said it 'cause it's what I think.

The phone rings. JEANNE looks at the others not knowing what to do.

GABRIEL
Don't answer. It's him.

MONIQUE
Or California. André, maybe it's Michel.

GABRIEL
Don't answer. If it's him.... Don't / answer. Don't answer.

SIMON
You gave him / this number...

MONIQUE
Yes.

JEANNE looks at GABRIEL.

JEANNE
It could be Montreal for Josée too.

ANDRÉ
If it's Michel, I'd really like to / know how...

GABRIEL
(It's him.) Okay, answer, answer.

JEANNE *(into the phone)*
Yes?

GABRIEL
Is it him?

JEANNE nods.

ANDRÉ *(to SIMON)*
You'll have to move the truck.

GABRIEL
Hang up.

SIMON
What does he want?

GABRIEL
Hang up.

SIMON
Don't you want to know what he wants?

JEANNE
He wants Louise. He wants to talk to…

GABRIEL
Gimme.

JEANNE *(into the phone)*
Just a second…. What?… Yes, but you'll have to wait.

GABRIEL
Gimme.

JEANNE
Gabriel…

GABRIEL
Gimme.

JEANNE
It's not worth it. What good's / it going to…?

GABRIEL
Okay, okay. Forget it.

SIMON
Ask him what he wants.

GABRIEL
What he wants? We know what he wants.

ANDRÉ *(to GABRIEL)*
The truck? Your pick-up truck? You'll have to…

GABRIEL
I'll do it when… I'll do it after.

ANDRÉ
Yes. It's just that / we can't…

GABRIEL
AFTER!

SIMON
André.

ANDRÉ
It's all right. I don't like to be spoken to like that / but it's all right.

GABRIEL
What does he want? Ask him what he wants.

JEANNE *(on the phone)*
Hello…? He's not there anymore. Hello…?

SIMON
Hang up.

JEANNE *(on the phone)*
No, her mother… yes, I know, but she can't come to the phone. Is there a message?

GABRIEL
Aw, fuck the message!

JEANNE
He wants her to call him back.

GABRIEL
(Hang up. Hang up on the bastard.)

JEANNE *(on the phone)*
She can't.
She can't that's all.
Why? / Because she can't.

GABRIEL *(to ANDRÉ)*
I'll move the truck. Okay? I'll move it. / I'm sorry for before.

JEANNE *(on the phone)*
Yes. Yes, she's waiting for you…. Is there a message? "It's because" what?

MONIQUE *(urgently, in a whisper)*
André!

ANDRÉ *(same)*
I'm coming!

JEANNE *(on the phone)*
No, wait…
(to SIMON)
Go get her.

SIMON
Louise?

JEANNE
Louise. Go get her.
(on the phone)
Hello?... Just a second...
(to SIMON)
Go on.

MONIQUE   *(low, to JEANNE)*
He's not coming?

JEANNE   *(to SIMON)*
Go get her!

>   *SIMON gets up and heads off in the direction of the cars.*

MONIQUE   *(low, to JEANNE)*
He's not coming, that's it, isn't it?

JEANNE   *(into the phone)*
She's coming.... Hello?... She's coming.

SIMON   *(calling)*
Louise!

JEANNE   *(into the phone)*
Hello?... We're calling her.

SIMON   *(calling)*
Louise!

JEANNE   *(into the phone)*
She's coming.

>   *GABRIEL suddenly rushes out in the direction of the cars.*

GABRIEL   *(yelling)*
Louise! TELEPHONE!

SIMON   *(shouting)*
Telephone!

>   *GABRIEL comes back signalling to JEANNE that LOUISE has heard them. He heads for the swing and throws himself into it.*

JEANNE   *(into the phone)*
   Hold on.

ANDRÉ   *(low)*
   Monique…

>   *MONIQUE nods. Then she goes to get her purse which is beside the swing. As she does, ANDRÉ speaks to SIMON.*

   We'll leave you the bottle.

SIMON
   No, really…

ANDRÉ
   It's open. Once it's open / it's not worth…

SIMON
   Jeanne, do we have a cork for…

ANDRÉ
   No, no, we're leaving it for you. *(to MONIQUE)* We'll leave them the shrimp too?

MONIQUE
   Yes, yes.

JEANNE
   Monique…

MONIQUE
   We can't take them, there's no fridge at the bed and breakfast. They'll go bad. Stink up the place.

JEANNE
   You could eat them.

MONIQUE
   Sshshsh.

ANDRÉ   *(to SIMON, low)*
   It's about the truck…

>   *SIMON nods. MONIQUE and ANDRÉ pick up the cooler. Then…*

MONIQUE   *(to JEANNE)*
   We…?

JEANNE
We'll call each other.

> MONIQUE and ANDRÉ exit in the direction of the cars as LOUISE comes back in with her suitcase. Then, once they've walked past her:

ANDRÉ (low)
You knew, didn't you? I know you did. It was obvious.

MONIQUE (low)
My brother talked to me about it / but I never thought...

ANDRÉ (low)
Not appreciated, Monique. You should've warned me. Definitely not appreciated!

> Then, as they exit:

MONIQUE (low)
Which way did the snake go?

> JEANNE puts the phone down on the table. LOUISE picks it up.

LOUISE (into the phone)
Yes?...
No?...
Hm...
(a quick explosive laugh)
What does it "imply"?
Hm, hm...

> LOUISE shuts her eyes. A pause. Then, LOUISE suddenly hangs up and throws the cordless on the table. Then, as she goes and pours herself a glass of champagne and without looking at the others, and very quickly:

Maybe we could erase what just happened and pick up where we left off. Go get Aunt Monique and Mr. Mathieu before they leave. Eat shrimp. Raise a glass to their wedding. Finish the bottle. Open another one. We could ask Mr. Mathieu to tell us all about California and his son and daughter-in-law. Earlier, while we were visiting the property, all he told me was that you could see the Pacific Ocean from their living room. Imagine. The Pacific.
(She realizes that Jeanne is shooting daggers at her with her eyes.)

(A short pause.)
The Pacific.

> *Suddenly, she doubles over seized by a wave of pain, anger and sobbing. She mutters to herself. Maybe we can make out: "He told me... the bastard... when we were..." But not much more than that.*
> *Then, it stops as quickly as it started. She continues.*

Everything's stopped for now. But someone—don't know who but someone—someone here, yes someone right here will eventually say something, something ah... normal. Something unimportant and perfectly... normal. Don't know who, don't know what. Don't know when. And then, another person here will answer or add something or finish what was started, and...
(pause) Okay. Maybe not right away.

> *ANDRÉ comes back in. It's pretty obvious he's had it with the present situation.*

ANDRÉ
Listen, I'm really very sorry, but I want to get out.
(no one moves)
Would someone please be good enough to let us out?
(same)
This is ridiculous. I'm not going to ask again. I've already asked I don't know how many times... (three, four at least...) This is no way to behave! You agree with me, don't you, Simon?

SIMON
Yes.

ANDRÉ
It's not done.

SIMON
We'll see to it.

ANDRÉ
I asked / politely...

SIMON
It's just that we're / right in the middle of...

ANDRÉ
...very politely!

SIMON
Yes.

ANDRÉ
Even in a situation like this. I understand you're upset, but even in a situation like this, it's just not done.

> *No one moves. MONIQUE comes back in from the direction of the cars. She's moving fast and has obviously made up her mind about something.*

MONIQUE
André, leave them be. / They'll come when…

ANDRÉ *(ignoring her)*
Even in situations like this, there's has to be a minimum of common courtesy. A minimum of… good manners!

SIMON
Yes.

ANDRÉ
Basic rules of behaviour that allow us to act, to interact, like human beings. Without them…

MONIQUE
André!

ANDRÉ
Monique, go back to the car! Go back to the car immediately! I'm handling this!
(to SIMON)
Isn't that what we were talking about, Simon? Isn't it? Basic rules of good behaviour?
Rules that mean we don't act like savages. Or lunatics. Or animals!

MONIQUE
André, come on…

ANDRÉ
Monique, I TOLD YOU TO GO BACK TO THE CAR!

> *Short pause. Then, as she crosses to GABRIEL:*

LOUISE
Give me the car key.

(to MONIQUE)
I'll leave. That way you two can get out.

ANDRÉ
Good!

LOUISE
Gimme. Give...

ANDRÉ
Good! It's about time!
(ANDRÉ heads in the direction of the cars. As he leaves, to MONIQUE:)
Come on.

MONIQUE doesn't follow him right away.

LOUISE
I want it. It's mine.

GABRIEL
Yours? Since when? The pick-up / is in your parent's names...

LOUISE
The key is mine. The truck is mine. What's in the truck / is mine...!

GABRIEL
You're going to let her get away with that! "Give me the key. The key is mine. The truck is mine. The place. The land. The equipment. The maple bush. The cows..."

LOUISE
(Stop, damn it! That's enough.)

GABRIEL
You know what I've done around here. Without me, you would've lost this place years ago. Without me...!? But now it's "Fuck you, Gaby" is that it?

JEANNE
It's not hers yet. Not the truck. Not the place.

LOUISE
Soon.

JEANNE
Soon, but not yet! Maybe not at all! / Maybe not ever!

SIMON
>Jeanne!
>*(to GABRIEL)*
>Give her the key, she'll give it back to you.

LOUISE
>No, I won't give it back to him because nothing's changed.
>*(to GABRIEL)*
>Let's take three days. Then, we'll talk.

>>*We hear a horn sound. This time, it's from ANDRÉ's car. The sound will be very loud and very aggressive and will go on intermittently – sometimes a series of short toots; sometimes long ones through what follows. The sounds will stop only briefly.*

>>*Pause. Then, taking the key out of his pocket, GABRIEL crosses up to the screen door, opens it and waits.*

>What?
>*(He throws the key inside. Horn.)*
>Shit, Gaby.

GABRIEL *(to MONIQUE)*
>Go tell him we're coming. It won't be long.

LOUISE *(as she goes inside)*
>Why'd you do that with the key?

GABRIEL
>Surprised you? Eh? Surprised you? That's why I did it.

>>*He follows her. The screen door slams shut. Then he closes the heavy front door behind them.*

>>*Horn. MONIQUE starts to exit in that direction, but changes her mind and comes back and picks up the brochure PAULETTE left on the chair.*

>>*The main door opens. LOUISE tries to come back out by pushing the screen door. But GABRIEL grabs her. She struggles. Pulls herself free for a moment. Pushes the screen door. He grabs her again this time by the hair. Crying out and at the same time as the horn:*

LOUISE
>NO! Ow! NO! I said No!

> *He puts his hand over her mouth. Pulls her back inside. The screen door slams shut. Then, the other door shuts with a loud bang.*
>
> *Several horn toots. In a state:*

MONIQUE
We really should go get the key. Right away.

JEANNE
We'll let them finish. They're talking.
(several toots of the horn)
They're just talking.
(We hear a thud coming from inside the house. SIMON starts to move toward the house. Stopping him:)
Isn't there one in the garage? A key? With all the others?

SIMON
Yes. But...

JEANNE
You'll be able to find it?

SIMON
Yes. There's a place where we keep all the duplicates.

> *Horn. A long one. JEANNE motions to SIMON to go and he leaves as quickly as possible in the direction of the barn. As he goes, he motions to ANDRÉ to be patient. The horn stops. MONIQUE moves over toward JEANNE, staring steadily at the closed front door as she does. JEANNE notices the brochure.*

JEANNE
Alaska. Isn't it too cold to go to Alaska in September? Mustn't be if the cruise ships are still going up there?

MONIQUE
Jeanne.

JEANNE *(taking the brochure from MONIQUE)*
I've never wanted to travel.

MONIQUE
Jeanne.

JEANNE
It must be beautiful though. Away.

MONIQUE
Jeanne.

JEANNE *(referring to the brochure)*
It must be beautiful, to see that live. The mountains. The whales.
(We hear another thud coming from inside the house.)
But I make do with photos. With films on TV. I know it's beautiful elsewhere but this... this is home and...
(putting down the brochure)
No doubt about it, must be nice to actually see something like that. Must be beautiful.

MONIQUE
Jeanne, don't you think that... we can't / let them...

JEANNE
I think we'd better forget about my little trip next week. There's too much work here this time of year. Guess you've forgotten that. You've been away in the city for so many years now.

MONIQUE
Jeanne, we can't just / let them ...

JEANNE
Your fiancé's waiting for you, you'd better go.

> *A long pause. MONIQUE looks off in the direction of the cars while PAULETTE comes back from the henhouse with her basket.*

PAULETTE
I've got seven!

MONIQUE
I'll go wait in the car with André.

JEANNE
Don't forget your brochure.
(MONIQUE leaves quickly without taking the brochure. PAULETTE heads for the house.)
Where are you going?

PAULETTE
I've got seven.

JEANNE
I'll take them in for you.

PAULETTE
Don't bother yourself. You've got guests. I gave the hens some water. Poor things.
Glad I wore my boots 'cause it's messy.

JEANNE
You'll have to put your shoes back on before you go in.

PAULETTE
I was going to! I never go into the house with my boots on. When did you ever see me go into the house with my boots on?

> *PAULETTE is about to go up onto the veranda.*

JEANNE
Can I see them?

> *Short pause.*

PAULETTE
They're eggs.

> *PAULETTE starts to take off her boots. SIMON comes back from where the cars are parked.*

SIMON
Done. Have you ever seen anything like it? He's a madman.

JEANNE
Sit down, Mother. In your chair. I'll take them in for you later.

> *During JEANNE's lines, the doors open. GABRIEL comes out and hurries off in the direction of the barn. He stops, comes back toward the house, changes his mind and starts to head back toward the barn again. But then, he grabs a chair, sits in it, cradles his head in his hands and starts to rock back and forth.*

(whispering)
Gabriel?
(LOUISE appears in the doorway. Her dress is torn. She's shaking. Wracked with trembling she can't control.)
Gaby?

PAULETTE
Lou-Lou, look at the eggs. I found seven. Nice big ones. For my omelette. The guests can have roast.

LOUISE
The... the guests... the guests are gone, Gran.

PAULETTE
Gone? And your dinner, Jeanne? Your roast?

> *LOUISE opens the screen door. She moves toward JEANNE in a daze. PAULETTE goes into the house in her stocking feet. The phone rings. Twice. SIMON answers.*

SIMON
Yes?...
No. They've left...
Yes. Do you have the number?...
A girl?
Oh. That's big.

> *GABRIEL gets up suddenly causing his chair to fall over. But he doesn't go anywhere.*

So, everything's fine in California?
Here? You wouldn't believe how hot it is here. Been almost a week now.

> *Through the living room window we can vaguely make out (but can't actually see) PAULETTE who's turned on her electric fan. Then we hear the same gospel music we heard at the beginning. It's played softly.*

The ocean?... Right... that's true. You've got the ocean.
Yeah, you've got to go, okay. I understand that.
But... Michel? You still there? Good.
I wanted to wish you... on behalf of all of us here... from the whole family here... from the bottom of our hearts...
Yeah, all right.
Yes.

> *SIMON hangs up.*
>
> *Silence.*
>
> *Blackout.*

Silence.

POST SHOW
AFTER THE FINAL CURTAIN CALL

Not long after the house lights come up, and while the first audience members are starting to leave the theatre... one of the chains holding up the swing gives way suddenly with a clatter making a lot of noise.

Then, we hear Emmylou Harris's version of the French song, "Plaisir d'Amour." ·

About the Author

Jean Marc Dalpé Three time recipient of the Governor General's literary award, Jean Marc Dalpé has written several highly acclaimed plays including *Le Chien*, *Ed-dy*, *Lucky Lady*, and *Trick or Treat*. After having lived for many years in Ontario, he now lives in Montreal with his partner Maureen Labonté and their daughter, Marielle.

About the Translator

Maureen Labonté is a dramaturge, translator and teacher. She has also coordinated a number of play development programmes in theatres and playwrights' centres across the country.

In 2006, she was named Head of Program for the Banff playRites Colony at the Banff Centre for the Arts. She was dramaturge at the Colony from 2003–2005. She was also Literary Manager in charge of play development at The Shaw Festival from 2002–2004. Previous to that, she worked at the National Theatre School of Canada, first developing and running a pilot Directing Programme and then coordinating the Playwrighting Programme and Playwrights' Residency. She still teaches at NTSC.

She has translated more than thirty Quebec plays into English. Recent translations include: *The Bookshop* by Marie-Josée Bastien, *Everybody's WELLES pour tous* by Patrice Dubois and Martin Labreque and *The Tailor's Will* by Michel Ouellette. She will soon be starting work on: *Wigwam* by Jean-Frédéric Messier and *Bienvenue à (une ville dont vous êtes le touriste)* by Olivier Choinière.